INDIA

BY TAMMY GAGNE

Essential Library
An Imprint of Abdo Publishing
abdobooks.com

ABDOBOOKS.COM
Published by Abdo Publishing, a division of ABDO, PO Box 398166, Minneapolis, Minnesota 55439.

Printed in the United States of America, North Mankato, Minnesota.
102022
012023

THIS BOOK CONTAINS RECYCLED MATERIALS

Cover Photos: Yury Taranik/Shutterstock Images (Taj Mahal); Tania Anisimova Design/Shutterstock Images (pattern)
Interior Photos: Tuul & Bruno Morandi/The Image Bank/Getty Images, 4–5; iStockphoto, 6, 21, 25, 56–57, 90–91; Shutterstock Images, 8, 15, 30, 45, 62, 76, 98; Nicole Kwiatkowski/Shutterstock Images, 9; Roop Dey/Shutterstock Images, 11; Photo 12/A7A collection/Alamy, 13; Riyas Net/Shutterstock Images, 16–17; Peter Hermes Furian/Shutterstock Images, 18 (India); Web Tools/Shutterstock Images, 18 (globe); Mazur Travel/Shutterstock Images, 23, 32–33; Joe McDonald/Shutterstock Images, 28–29; Tanes Ngamsom/iStockphoto, 35; Ondrej Prosicky/Shutterstock Images, 37; Puttachat Kumkrong/Shutterstock Images, 38; Vadim Petrakov/Shutterstock Images, 40–41; Morten Svenningsen/Alamy, 42; Deepak Bishnoi/Shutterstock Images, 44; Poltu Shyamal/Shutterstock Images, 47; Ian Dagnall Computing/Alamy, 51; World History Archive/Alamy, 53; Nasir Kachroo/Nur Photo/Getty Images, 55; Daniel Rao/iStockphoto, 58; Joshua Resnick/Shutterstock Images, 61; Snehal Jeevan Pailkar/Shutterstock Images, 63; Dibyangshu Sarkar/AFP/Getty Images, 64; Fine Art Images/Heritage Images/Hulton Archive/Getty Images, 66; Stephane Cardinale/Corbis Entertainment/Getty Images, 67; Yoda Mclaren/Shutterstock Images, 69; Florian Augustin/Shutterstock Images, 70–71; Partha Sarkar/Xinhua News Agency/Getty Images, 72; Manpreet Romana/AFP/Getty Images, 75; Henri Bureau/Corbis/VCG/Sygma/Getty Images, 77; Sam Panthaky/AFP/Getty Images, 78; Jaya Kumar/Shutterstock Images, 80–81; Arun Sankar/AFP/Getty Images, 82–83; CDS Photography/Shutterstock Images, 84; De Visu/Shutterstock Images, 87; Leonid Andronov/iStockphoto, 89; CRS Photo/Shutterstock Images, 94; Pep Roig/Alamy, 95; V. S. Anandhakrishna/Shutterstock Images, 99; T. Lesia/Shutterstock Images, 101

Editor: Priscilla An
Series Designer: Maggie Villaume

Library of Congress Control Number: 2022940306

PUBLISHER'S CATALOGING-IN-PUBLICATION DATA
Names: Gagne, Tammy, author.
Title: India / by Tammy Gagne
Description: Minneapolis, Minnesota: Abdo Publishing, 2023 | Series: Essential Library of Countries | Includes online resources and index.
Identifiers: ISBN 9781532199424 (lib. bdg.) | ISBN 9781098274627 (ebook)
Subjects: LCSH: India--Juvenile literature. | Asia--Juvenile literature. | India--History--Juvenile literature. | Geography--Juvenile literature.
Classification: DDC 954--dc23

CONTENTS

CHAPTER **ONE**

A TOUR OF INDIA

Gina had dreamed of visiting India her whole life. Although Gina was born in the United States, her mother had been born and raised in a small town in India called Mathura. It is known for being the birthplace of Krishna. Gina's mother told her many stories about the highly revered Hindu god and the many temples that honored him. She also spoke fondly of the Taj Mahal in nearby Agra. People traveled from all over India and the rest of the world to visit the elaborate building. Now Gina was going to spend part of her summer vacation with her mother's family in India. She was excited to see where her mother grew up and go to the places that meant

Krishna is one of the major gods in Hinduism, the most common religion in India.

Indira Gandhi International Airport features an installation of large resin hands. Each hand is folded into a different mudra, or hand gesture, that is popular in classical Indian dance forms.

so much to her mother. She also looked forward to meeting her maternal grandparents for the first time.

When Gina arrived at Indira Gandhi International Airport in New Delhi, she searched the crowd for Uncle Samir and Aunt Maya. She hoped her cousin Sara would come with them to pick her up. Gina had met them all when they visited California a few years earlier. She remembered being surprised by how much she and Sara had in common despite coming from such different cultures. They both loved listening to music, watching movies, and scrolling through Instagram.

Gina smiled when she saw three familiar faces approaching. When Samir took Gina's suitcase in his right hand, she remembered what her mother told her about Indian etiquette. Touching people or picking up objects with one's left hand is considered disrespectful. Maya and Sara hugged Gina hello. They asked about her flight, and she told them she had slept on the long ride from Los Angeles. It was early morning in India, and she was well rested for her first day with them.

Gina assured her family she was hungry as they headed home together for breakfast with Nani and Nana. Like other grandchildren in India, Gina called her maternal grandmother and grandfather by these names. Although they had never met face-to-face, Gina spoke to her grandparents on the phone and through video calls often. Kids in India used different names for their paternal grandparents. Because Nani and Nana were Samir's parents, Sara called them Dadi and Dada.

Nani had made stuffed parathas, a popular Indian breakfast, to celebrate Gina's arrival. She had prepared the dough the previous evening, letting it rise overnight. Gina caught the enticing scent as soon as she stepped through the doorway of the family's home. Nani told her she had made both aloo paratha and methi paratha. Aloo paratha was stuffed with potatoes, while the methi paratha was filled with fenugreek, an herb that smelled like maple syrup. When Gina asked for one of each, Nani seemed pleased. Gina soon learned a methi paratha tasted like maple syrup too. Her mother often made traditional Indian foods at home, but this one was a delightful new treat.

Methi paratha can be served with pickle and curd.

After breakfast, Maya announced that the first stop on Gina's tour of India would be the Taj Mahal. She asked if Gina brought an umbrella, reminding her that monsoon season had just begun. It frequently rained between midmorning and late afternoon in India throughout July until September. Maya said they had extra umbrellas if she needed one, but Gina's mother had tucked one in her suitcase when they packed for her trip.

THE TAJ MAHAL

The Mughal emperor Shah Jahan built the Taj Mahal mausoleum to honor his late wife, Mumtaz Mahal, after she died in childbirth in 1631. He spared no expense building the extravagant complex, which is considered one of the most beautiful and most expensive pieces of architecture in the world. Shah Jahan spent 32 million rupees to build the Taj Mahal.[1] That is the equivalent of nearly $1 billion today.

The Taj Mahal is a popular site for tourists. Each year, approximately seven to eight million people visit the Taj Mahal, and 800,000 of these tourists are from around the world.

Consisting largely of white marble, the structure is decorated in elaborate designs made from semiprecious gemstones. Millions of tourists visit the Taj Mahal each year.

Gina had seen many photos of the Taj Mahal over the years. She wondered if it would be as amazing in real life as it seemed. Thankfully, the sun was high up in the sky with no sign of clouds or rainfall. The grand palace was glowing a brilliant white in the sun, making Gina squint her eyes. When she walked through the main gate, she knew exactly why the Taj Mahal became a UNESCO World Heritage site in 1983. UNESCO stands for United Nations Educational, Scientific, and Cultural Organization. The UNESCO World Heritage Committee chooses sites that have outstanding cultural value for this designation. The Taj Mahal was every bit as breathtaking as Gina imagined. She marveled at the intricate patterns and elegant Arabic calligraphy inscribed on the marble walls.

They also visited two more World Heritage sites nearby, the Agra Fort and Fatehpur Sikri. Also known as the Red Fort of Agra, the Agra Fort was constructed of red sandstone. Its towering walls have a circumference of approximately 1.5 miles (2.5 km).[2] Gina remarked that Agra Fort was like a small city. Samir explained that Mughal emperor Akbar commissioned the fort to protect his imperial city within it. Huge palaces, mosques, and audience halls still stand within the fort.

It took 20,000 workers to build the Taj Mahal mausoleum. The entire complex, which covers 42 acres (17 ha), took 22 years to complete.[3]

As the family began touring Fatehpur Sikri, Gina asked what this city, mostly constructed of red sandstone, had been built for. Although it lacked

Fatehpur Sikri means "city of victory." The city was made the capital in the 1500s but only for about ten years.

the ornateness of the Taj Mahal, it was as striking as the Agra Fort. Maya explained that Fatehpur Sikri is even older than the two other landmarks they'd visited that day. It was built in the late 1500s by Akbar, who made the city his capital. As Gina and her family finished exploring for the day, she realized how tired she was getting. Her first day in India seemed to fly by, but jet lag was catching up with her.

BOLLYWOOD AND MORE

Back home, Maya asked Gina how she would like to spend the next day. The family had made a basic itinerary for Gina's visit, but they left some empty space in it. They wanted to make sure they included activities that Gina might have in mind, as well as the things they hoped she would enjoy doing.

Sara quickly suggested going to a theater to see a Bollywood film. Gina knew that the Bollywood film industry was popular in India. Sara often spoke passionately about the movies it produced. Gina had seen that Sara followed many popular Bollywood stars, such as Ananya Panday and Shahid Kapoor, on social media.

A BOOMING FILM INDUSTRY

The popularity of Bollywood films extends far beyond India. This film industry comes in second only to Hollywood in making money internationally. Bollywood beats Hollywood when it comes to quantity, though. Bollywood releases more films each year than any film industry in the world.

The name Bollywood is a portmanteau. This means it was created by combining two other words—in this case, *Bombay* and *Hollywood*. Based in Mumbai, a city formerly known as Bombay, Bollywood is like the Hollywood of India.

Although Gina wanted to share the experience of a Bollywood film with her cousin, she wasn't sure about it. She confessed that she wouldn't be able to follow a Bollywood movie's storyline. While her family spoke both Hindi and English fluently, Gina could speak only a small amount

The popular 2001 Bollywood film *Lagaan: Once Upon a Time in India* stars Aamir Khan and Gracy Singh.

of Hindi. She didn't think a movie would be much fun if she didn't understand the dialogue. Sara and Maya exchanged a knowing smile at Gina's concern.

"You don't have to worry," Maya explained. "Most Bollywood films are made in Hindi, but

The Bollywood film industry releases between 1,500 and 2,000 movies each year.[4]

theaters offer showings with English subtitles for the most popular films." Gina agreed that it sounded like a good idea, so Sara looked up which movies were playing with subtitles the next day. Observing the conversation, Samir noticed that Gina seemed a little disappointed.

"Was there something else you would like to do tomorrow as well?" he asked.

Gina shared that she had hoped to visit one of her mother's favorite temples, but she didn't know which one. She had looked some up while she was waiting at the airport, and the sheer number of temples in the area was overwhelming.

Samir suggested one nearby called Baba Jaigurudev Mandir. He and Gina's mother used to visit this temple as teenagers. He admitted that it wasn't the most famous, but Gina's mother loved that the entire structure was a brilliant white. She had always said it made the temple look like the Taj Mahal. Gina said it sounded like a perfect choice. Exploring India was proving to be an exhausting but thrilling journey.

HINDU TEMPLES

Hindu temples are sacred places built to honor the gods. Visitors are expected to show respect to the gods in several ways. They should always arrive clean and modestly dressed. Although specifics vary from one temple to another, this typically means abstaining from wearing shorts or showing one's shoulders. Visitors should also remove their shoes before entering a temple. Many temples have brass bells near their entrances. Visitors are expected to ring these bells to notify the gods of their arrival, similar to the way they would knock on the door of a person's home.

THE NATION OF INDIA

India is one of the largest countries in the world, both in area and by population. It has a long and intricate history. India is considered the birthplace of many of the world's most widespread religions, including Buddhism and Hinduism. Hinduism is the most common religion of India today.

Indian culture includes a vast array of art, architecture, clothing, food, and more. Its tourism industry offers visitors a wide variety of historical sites and natural wonders. The nation has more than 100 national parks with exotic plants and animals, some of which are on the world's endangered species list.[5] India has 22 official languages, including Hindi, the world's oldest language.[6] Its diversity, culture, and history make India a fascinating place for all who explore it.

THE SACRED COW

The phrase "sacred cow" has come to mean any idea or custom that is protected at all costs. The phrase comes from the Hindu custom of protecting cows, as cows are considered sacred. In the Hindu religion, cows represent the maternal attributes of goddesses. One way that Hindus show their respect for this animal is by not eating beef. Killing a cow for any reason is a crime in many states in India.

CHAPTER **TWO**

GEOGRAPHY

India is the seventh-largest country in the world. It covers more than 1.2 million square miles (3.2 million sq km).[1] A wide variety of terrain is found in the nation, including salt deserts, forests teeming with wildlife, and some of the world's tallest mountains. India's lakes and rivers draw visitors to the country for many reasons, from spiritual to recreational.

India has land borders with six other countries. Pakistan, which was once part of India, lies to the northwest. Nepal, China, and Bhutan are to the north. Bangladesh and Myanmar border India to the east. The island nation of Sri Lanka is located just 40 miles (65 km) off India's southeastern coast in the Gulf of Mannar.[2] India, Pakistan, and Bangladesh together are often referred to as the Indian subcontinent. This part

There are many types of landscapes in India, such as the Kerala Backwaters, a network of lakes, canals, and lagoons in southern India.

MAP OF INDIA

KEY:
- Capital
- City
- Point of Interest

of southern Asia is set apart from the rest of the continent by the Himalayas and several other large mountain ranges.

India has 29 states. The largest state is Rajasthan, which is in the western part of the country bordering Pakistan. It measures 132,139 square miles (342,239 sq km).[3] The nation's smallest state is Goa, located in the southeast. It covers just 1,429 square miles (3,702 sq km).[4] Each state has a legislature that works with the central government of India. The country also has eight union territories. Most of these are controlled directly by the national government. Two of India's union territories do have their own legislatures, however. They are Delhi and Puducherry. The capital city of New Delhi is in the north-central part of the country. Other large cities include Bengaluru, Kolkata, and Mumbai.

The state of Rajasthan makes up more than 10 percent of India's land.[6]

MOUNTAINS

Part of the Himalayas, Mount Kanchenjunga is India's tallest mountain at 28,169 feet (8,586 m).[5] It is the third-highest peak in the world. Mount Kanchenjunga is in the state of Sikkim in the northeastern part of India near the border to Nepal. Although Nepal's Mount Everest is better known because it is the world's tallest peak, many climbers consider Mount Kanchenjunga to be equally challenging. This is because of the high unpredictability of snowstorms and avalanches on the mountain. Even climbers who have reached the top of Everest still want to climb Mount Kanchenjunga.

The Purvanchal Range forms the boundary between India and Myanmar. Compared to the peaks in the Himalayas, this range is low. The average peak height is 9,845 feet (3,001 m) above sea level.[7] Although this range doesn't attract as many tourists as the Himalayas, the views are particularly scenic near the Myanmar border. Nature lovers also enjoy the wildlife found in Namdapha National Park in the state of Arunachal Pradesh and Keibul Lamjao National Park in the state of Manipur, which are both located along the Purvanchal Range. Namdapha is the only national park in the country that has four large cat species. Leopards, clouded leopards, snow leopards, and tigers are all found there. Keibul Lamjao National Park is the only place in the wild where the sangai deer species live.

The Aravalli Range is in the eastern part of the country. Most of this range is in the state of Rajasthan. Its highest peak is Guru Shikhar, which has an elevation of 5,650 feet (1,722 m).[8] The range borders the Thar Desert, protecting much of Rajasthan from the desert's harsh climate.

MOUNTAIN TEMPERATURES

The coldest winter temperatures on India's mountains vary dramatically between ranges. In January, the lowest temperatures in the Purvanchal Mountains dip to 41 degrees Fahrenheit (5°C).[9] This is a far cry from the low of –22 degrees Fahrenheit (–30°C) that winter can bring to Mount Kanchenjunga.[10] The reasons for this vast temperature difference are the ranges' different altitudes and latitudes. Air is colder at higher elevations and when a location is farther from the equator.

On a clear day, the snowy peaks of Mount Kanchenjunga can be seen from the city of Darjeeling.

The Aravalli Range is among the oldest inhabited areas of the world. Archeologists have found evidence that there were people in this region in 2500 BCE or earlier. Many forts and palaces constructed during the land's long history still stand today. They make the mountain range an interesting tourist attraction.

DESERTS

The Thar Desert in Rajasthan is one of the world's largest deserts, spanning an area of more than 77,000 square miles (200,000 sq km).[11] In the summer, temperatures in the desert can rise to more than 122 degrees Fahrenheit (50°C), but winter temperatures often drop to near freezing. Like other deserts, the Thar gets minimal rain—less than four inches (10.2 cm) each year in the west and 20 inches (50.8 cm) in the east.[12] Though people might consider this ecoregion to be uninhabitable because of its harsh temperatures, the Thar Desert is the most densely populated desert in the world. About 40 percent of Rajasthan's population call the desert home.[13] People have lived in this area for thousands of years. While many deserts are desolate places, the Thar Desert includes numerous roads and other infrastructure such as railways and airports.

THE TWO REGIONS OF THE RANN

The Rann of Kachchh is divided into two distinctive desert regions, the Great Rann of Kachchh and the Little Rann of Kachchh. The Great Rann is one large expanse of salt. The Little Rann of Kachchh is interspersed with salt-free areas. Known as bets, these salt-free areas provide habitats to 32 different mammal species.

In the Thar Desert, camels are a common mode of transportation.

Another notable desert in India is the Rann of Kachchh in Gujarat. This desert is southwest of the Thar Desert. It is often referred to as the Great Salt Desert because of the sandy white salt that covers the ground. The Rann of Kachchh is a striking sight. Some visitors say it looks like a plain of diamonds shining under the sky day and night. For centuries, this region was submerged in the Arabian Sea, but an earthquake shifted the plain above sea level. The salt extends dozens of feet below the ground's surface. During monsoon season, seawater returns to the region. As it recedes in October, salt farmers harvest this abundant natural resource.

FORESTS

Gir Forest is also located in Gujarat. The land has been protected as a game preserve since 1913, when it was first used to save rare Asiatic lions. When Gir National Park was created in 1965, the forest became part of that protected space as well. Gir Forest consists of a variety of dry, deciduous trees including dhak, sal, and teak. The trees provide essential habitats for many birds and other animals.

In the state of West Bengal in eastern India, the Sundarbans is another forest that provides important refuge to wildlife. This mangrove forest is a reserve for Bengal tigers and a host of other animals and plants. It is also the largest connected mangrove forest in the world. Sundari trees are the predominant species in the forest. These trees, which often measure six feet (1.8 m) across, can grow as high as 60 feet (18.2 m) tall.[14]

Kanha National Park in Madhya Pradesh includes many types of forests, including moist peninsular sal forests and southern tropical dry deciduous mixed forests. These environments allow a variety of animals to live and thrive. Visitors can see mammals like barasinghas, tigers, sloth bears, and leopards during jungle safari tours.

MAJOR WATERWAYS

The longest river in India, the Ganges, flows more than 1,569 miles (2,525 km) from the Himalayas to the Bay of Bengal.[15] People rely on this river for a variety of purposes. It is a water source for farming and everyday life in multiple states. Many industries depend on the river's hydroelectric dams, which produce power for a range of businesses.

The Ganges is often called India's holiest river. Hindus from all over the country travel great distances to visit temples and shrines that have been built along this river's banks. They call the river *Ganga Ma*, which means "Mother Ganges." Most Hindus try to make a pilgrimage to the Ganges at least once during their lives to bathe in its water. Drinking from the river is also said to bring good fortune.

Covering 785 square miles (2,033 sq km), the largest lake in India is Vembanad Lake in Kerala.[16]

Many Hindus bathe in the waters of the Ganges River.

A village called Kumarakom is situated on the east side of the lake. It is a popular destination for tourists who enjoy birdwatching, photography, and boating. Even people who know little about boating enjoy touring Vembanad Lake on traditional houseboats with thatched roofs and wooden hulls.

COASTLINE AND ISLANDS

The southern portion of the country forms a large peninsula. Nine of India's states and four of its union territories have land along the coast. The coastline is divided into two sections. There is the western coastline, which borders the Arabian Sea, and the eastern coastline, which borders the Bay of Bengal. The country's southernmost point marks the boundary between these two bodies of water.

India has more than 1,200 islands off its coast. The biggest group in the Arabian Sea is called Lakshadweep. It has 36 islands, all known for their sandy beaches, tropical climate, and crystal-clear lagoons. Lakshadweep means "a hundred thousand islands" in Malayalam and Sanskrit. Andrott Island is the largest Lakshadweep island. It has an area of approximately two square miles (5 sq km), and it is the closest island to the country's mainland.[17]

CLIMATE

Most of India has a tropical climate with four distinct seasons. Interior parts of the country experience a mix of wet and dry weather. Northern India is more humid than most other regions of the country. But a village called Mawsynram in the eastern state of Meghalaya is the wettest area. It gets more than 433 inches (1,100 cm) of rain each year.[18]

Although India has reputation for being relentlessly hot, temperatures vary by the season. Summer begins in March and can include temperatures as high as 104 degrees Fahrenheit (40°C). Monsoon season, which spans July to September, brings about three-quarters of India's annual rainfall. Autumn lasts from October to December. Both the heat and humidity lessen gradually during this milder period. Once December arrives, winter can begin anytime, bringing with it temperatures as cool as 50 degrees Fahrenheit (10°C) in the northwest and 68 degrees Fahrenheit (20°C) in the southeast.[19] In higher northern elevations, such as the Himalayas, the air temperature can drop far below freezing around this time. This area also receives significant snow.

WHAT IS A MONSOON?

Monsoon season is named for the weather pattern that brings large amounts of rain, humidity, and thunderstorms. There is a common misconception that a monsoon is a storm similar to a hurricane or typhoon. Although it does bring heavy winds and rain, a monsoon has a much broader weather pattern. India's summer monsoon season is typically from June to September and spans the entire country.

CHAPTER **THREE**

PLANTS AND ANIMALS

Many of India's plant and animal species are among the most beautiful and unusual in the world. In addition to serving important roles in the country's ecosystems, numerous species are also part of Indian culture. However, some of these plants and animals are at risk of extinction.

THE LOTUS

India's national flower is the lotus. This aquatic plant is native to southern Asia and Australia, and it can grow in a wide range of climates. The lotus grows in marshes, lagoons, and ponds. Its stem rises through the water, and its wide, disk-shaped leaves sit on or hover over

The barasingha is an endangered species of deer that can be found in central and northern India.

The lotus is an important symbol in Hinduism and Buddhism.

the surface. The eye-catching blossom atop the leaves can grow as wide as eight inches (20 cm) in diameter.[1] It can be blue, pink, purple, red, or white. Lotus leaves do not absorb water. Any water that falls on them simply beads up and slides off them due to their waxy exterior. People often call this "the lotus effect."

Hindus have long revered the lotus. To them, it symbolizes beauty, prosperity, and fertility. Hindu mythology is filled with stories that feature this plant. One of the most prominent myths tells a story of the lotus being created from the navel of the god Vishnu. The god Brahma was then born from the flower. This story has led many people to view the flower as a symbol of the universe itself.

The lotus is also sacred to Buddhists. They see the flower as a symbol of the highest state of human consciousness. Like the lotus, the most highly evolved Buddhists are said to grow pure in the sunlight with their heads held high and their feet rooted in experience. In many depictions of Buddha, he sits on top of a throne made of a lotus flower.

FLOWER OF HAPPINESS

Buddhism teaches that the lotus brings happiness. The roots of the lotus lie in mud, but no matter how dirty the water gets, the flower produces clean and beautiful petals. Like the lotus, Buddhists are encouraged to bring others happiness no matter how adverse their surrounding circumstances are.

BANYAN TREE

The banyan tree looks like a group of smaller trees that have grown together, but it is actually one massive tree. Also called the Indian fig tree, this sprawling plant is India's national tree. Although it also grows in Pakistan and the states of Florida and Hawaii in the United States, the banyan tree originated in India. A typical banyan tree can grow up to 100 feet (30 m) tall, but the more impressive measurement is the area that its roots can cover.[2]

The branches of the banyan tree grow roots that extend down to the ground, giving these roots the appearance of new tree trunks. As the tree continues to spread its roots, its footprint can

Banyan trees have a huge network of roots.

cover multiple acres of land. This process has made the banyan the world's largest tree in terms of area. The largest known banyan tree grows in Kolkata and spreads across five acres (2 ha).[3]

Like the lotus, the banyan tree has cultural significance in Indian mythology and religion. It is associated with several Hindu gods. The tree's bark is said to have come from Lord Vishnu, its branches from Lord Shiva, and its roots from Lord Brahma. The trees' leaves are said to be the resting place of the Hindu god Krishna. Many Indians view the banyan tree as possessing magical powers, including the ability to fulfill wishes.

The famous banyan tree in Kolkata, known for being the oldest of its kind, is more than 250 years old.[5]

ENDANGERED PLANT SPECIES

More than 300 of India's plant and tree species are endangered, meaning their numbers have dropped to the point of possible extinction.[4] One of these species is Malabar mahogany, which grows in Kerala, Karnataka, and Tamil Nadu. This tree is known for growing especially straight and tall. Some Malabar mahogany trees reach heights up to 197 feet (60 m).[6] The tree's wood is also extremely durable, making it a popular choice for lumber and furniture manufacturing.

Unfortunately, much of the land where Malabar mahogany trees once grew has been developed over time. The overharvesting and destruction of habitat have contributed to the species becoming endangered. Despite the tree's dwindling populations, wood manufacturing companies continue to harvest it. They can sell it for high prices to cabinet and furniture makers.

ELEPHANTS

The Asian elephant, also called the Indian elephant, is another popular symbol in Indian culture and religion. Ganesha, the Hindu god of new beginnings, has an elephant's head. Myths about Ganesha have created an image of the elephant as a remover of obstacles. Each elephant feature symbolizes different virtues to Hindus. The head represents wisdom and knowledge. The eyes are said to have the ability to see the future and recognize truth. The large ears stand for a talent of listening carefully, and the long trunk can sniff out both good and evil.

It takes a lot of food to fuel an Asian elephant. This animal can eat up 441 pounds (200 kg) of vegetation each day.[7]

The Asian elephant's ears are indeed quite large, but they are smaller than the ears of the African elephant. An elephant's ears help the animal

Female Asian elephants are very social and usually form groups of six or seven.

disperse heat, and, while hot at times, the Indian climate is less intense than in the regions of Africa where elephants live. The Asian species is also set apart by the single finger on its trunk tip. The African species has two of these fingers.

Asian elephants roam India's forests. Most are found in the country's tropical deciduous forests. These immense creatures and their African cousins are the heaviest terrestrial mammals on the planet. Adults stand as tall as 11 feet (3 m) and weigh up to six tons (5 metric tons).[8] Asian elephants eat a variety of forest vegetation including grasses, leaves, roots, and tree bark.

SLOTH BEAR

One might imagine that sloth bears, with their black, shaggy coats, would feel uncomfortable in India's tropical climate. But these big bears stay relatively cool. This is because the sloth bear's fur lacks the undercoat that many other bear species have. Unlike the more rotund Indian black bear that is also found in the country, the sloth bear has a lanky body. This doesn't stop it from reaching a formidable size, however. Sloth bears can measure as long as six feet (1.8 m) and weigh up to 308 pounds (140 kg).[9]

Sloth bears are found throughout India, southern Nepal, and Sri Lanka. They feast on a variety of insects in this region, including beetles, grubs, and termites. The bear's nose and mouth are adapted to its diet. Whereas most bears have two front teeth on top, the sloth bear does not. The extra space helps the bear suck up insects. The animal can also close its nostrils, which keeps dust and dirt from getting in the way when it sucks up its prey. Sloth bears also eat fruits such as figs and mangoes when they are in season.

RED PANDA

The state animal of Sikkim, the red panda is a small but energetic creature. Standing about 24 inches (61 cm) tall, even the largest red pandas weigh up to 17 pounds (7.7 kg).[10] Despite its name, this species is not closely related to the giant panda of China. The red panda was given the name, which comes from the Nepali word *ponya,* meaning "bamboo- or plant-eating animal," about 50 years before the black-and-white pandas were named.

Red pandas are very flexible and are skilled at climbing.

In addition to Sikkim, red pandas live in Arunachal Pradesh, Meghalaya, southern China, and West Bengal. They inhabit forests, where they spend most of their time in trees. They use their long, bushy tails for balance as they jump from branch to branch. They also have an extra thumb that they use for climbing and feeding. The red panda's diet consists almost exclusively of bamboo leaves. When bamboo shoots are in season, it will eat those as well.

ENDANGERED ANIMAL SPECIES IN INDIA

India has many endangered animal species. The Asian elephant and the red panda are included on this list. Another endangered species found in India is the Asiatic lion. This animal is a subspecies of the same large cat species as the African lion. At one time, these lions were found in parts of Europe, Africa, and Asia. Now, the Asiatic lion is found only in India. Only about 500 of these cats remain.[11]

The Bengal tiger's numbers are slightly higher, but they are still low enough for the species to be considered endangered. In 2020, about 2,000 of these large, striped cats still lived in India. This is about 70 percent of the total number left in the

PROTECTED SPACE FOR BENGAL TIGERS

Sundarbans National Park in West Bengal includes one of the largest tiger reserves in the world. More than 400 tigers live in this protected space.[12] Although the park was established in 1984, the area was developed as a wildlife sanctuary in 1977. Visitors to the park have an excellent chance of seeing one or more of these large cats while exploring the mangrove forest that the park also protects.

world.[13] Many of the Indian Bengal tiger populations are found in Corbett National Park in Uttarakhand.

The one-horned rhinoceros, also called the Indian rhinoceros, has been hunted for its horn. Traditional Chinese medicine has used rhino horns for centuries to treat a wide range of conditions. Since the animal became endangered, however, hunting it has become illegal in most places. Still, poachers continue to kill rhinos for their horns, pushing the species' population down even further. In 2020, about 2,000 Indian rhinos remained in the wild.[14] They live in the foothills of the Himalayas in both India and Nepal.

STAGGERING STRAY DOG POPULATION

India has a massive problem with stray dogs. As many as 40 million homeless dogs roam the streets of the nation.[15] Animal welfare organizations feed and vaccinate as many of the animals as they can. They also try to find them homes. The Rajasthan police have adopted some of the animals to train as canine officers. Most often, however, the dogs end up neglected or mistreated by people who fear them.

CHAPTER **FOUR**

HISTORY

People first came from Africa to the region now known as India as many as 65,000 years ago. Several civilizations have lived in India ever since. The Indus valley civilization was located in northern India and present-day Pakistan. Beginning around 5,000 years ago, it was the first urban civilization in India and one of the most extensive civilizations in the world. It included more than 1,400 small cities and towns.[1]

Many people lived along the Indus River. They used its water for drinking, washing, and growing crops. Archeologists think this civilization was peaceful. They have found very few weapons from this time in the region. Therefore, it is assumed that the Indus valley civilization didn't even have an army.

The Indus River is an important resource to communities that live near it. It is also one of the longest rivers in the world.

The Vedas are the most significant texts in Hinduism.

VEDIC PERIOD

The Vedic Period is named for the Vedic Sanskrit texts, called Vedas, which are believed to have been written between 1500 and 500 BCE. A group of scholars known as the Aryans traveled to India during this time from the region now known as Iran. Hindus believe Aryan scholars transcribed the texts directly from God. These works became the foundation for Hinduism.

The Vedic period brought many changes to Indian culture. Rules for marriage and basic family life were established during this time. Men became the leaders of Indian society. Kings ruled the civilization, while husbands led their families. Parents prayed to have sons.

Farming became increasingly popular during the Vedic period. This was how most people made a living. Several large kingdoms were created throughout the subcontinent as owning land became more important.

MAURYAN EMPIRE

Of all India's civilizations, the largest by far was the Mauryan Empire (321–185 BCE). The first major empire in the land, it was founded by Chandragupta Maurya. Before its formation, a corrupt king named Dhana Nanda ruled what is now part of eastern India. His kingdom, which was one of many in the region at the time, was called Magadha. When a scholar named Chanakya visited Magadha, Dhana Nanda insulted him. Chanakya vowed to get revenge. He convinced Chandragupta Maurya to raise an army and take the throne from Dhana Nanda. The war was bloody but swift, as many of Dhana Nanda's own men were willing to join Chandragupta Maurya in his fight against their oppressive ruler.

Over time, Chandragupta expanded his new kingdom. His son, Bindusara, took over the throne after Chandragupta's death. Bindusara continued conquests in the south, but he is best known as being the father of Ashoka the Great, the empire's third and final emperor. Ashoka expanded the Mauryan Empire even farther than his father

According to the ancient Roman author Pliny, Chandragupta's army was immense. It included 600,000 infantry, 30,000 cavalry, and 9,000 elephants.[2]

King Ashoka, one of the most influential kings in the Mauryan Empire, built the Great Stupa. This building is one of the oldest Buddhist monuments in India.

and grandfather. The empire now controlled most of the Indian subcontinent and beyond. It stretched north to south from the Himalayas to Sri Lanka, and east to west from Bangladesh to Afghanistan. Ashoka was highly revered for this accomplishment, but he developed deep regret over the carnage that his conquest demanded. As a result, he embraced Buddhism and introduced many of his subjects to the emerging, peaceful religion.

INDIA'S BUDDHIST ERA AND GANDHARA CULTURE

King Ashoka was revered even more in death than during his lifetime. His strong devotion to Buddhism became a focus of many legends about him. These stories inspired more people to practice Buddhism over the next several centuries. Buddhism became a leading religion in

Buddhism's influence can be seen in the many Buddhist temples and relics in India.

India during this time. Even many Hindus adopted the practices of Buddhism, viewing Buddha as an incarnation of the Hindu god Vishnu.

Between 300 BCE and 200 CE, India's culture began changing again. Traders traveled to India from Asia, Europe, and Persia. Most of these traders passed through an area called Gandhara in what is now Pakistan. The travelers shared their religions, art forms, and ideas about life with the Indian people. It didn't take long for new customs to spread throughout northern India. Buddhism remained popular. But its traditions mingled with those of China, Iran, and the Roman Empire.

Greece in particular had a major effect on Buddhist art. When Buddhism first emerged, most paintings and sculptures of Buddha did not show him in human form. Instead, artists used symbols associated with him. A tree, a wheel, or footprints were often used to represent him. But as Greek culture spread through India, more artists depicted Buddha as a person. Sometimes, even Greek deities were incorporated into Buddhist art. Greek gods, such as Atlas and Boreas, were depicted beside Buddha.

By 1100 CE, devotion to Buddhism had lessened significantly. Some historians think the reason was Buddhism's tolerance for other faiths. This made it easy for other religions, such as Hinduism, to add some Buddhist beliefs and practices as their own. Other historians point out that the decline of Buddhism may have been the result of a class conflict. As Buddhist monasteries accumulated great wealth, they began relying on enslaved people for the care of monks and the upkeep of monasteries. This likely made many of India's poorest Buddhists feel disconnected from the religion and more open to other faiths.

Many Muslims travel to Jama Masjid Mosque in Old Delhi, India, to pray during Eid al-Fitr, a day marking the end of Ramadan.

MUSLIM RULE OF INDIA

A Turkish tribe called the Ghaznavids invaded the area of India now known as Punjab in the 1100s CE. By 1200, much of northern India was ruled by the tribe's Muslim empire, known as the Delhi sultanate, which introduced the religion of Islam to the region. Its rulers conquered Hindu kingdoms as far south as modern-day Tamil Nadu.

In 1519, a ruler named Babur began launching raids in the Punjab region to expand his Mughal Empire from present-day Afghanistan into northern India. Babur continued his campaigns until his death in 1530, when his son Humayun took over the task, ultimately conquering the Delhi sultanate. Humayun's son Akbar extended the Mughal Empire throughout the subcontinent during his reign. Although the Mughals did not force the Indians to convert to Islam, the Muslim population increased substantially under their rule. Many people adopted the faith when they married a Muslim person. Others simply decided to convert to Islam on their own.

Akbar was just 13 years old when he was crowned as the third Mughal emperor.

BRITISH COLONIALISM

Portuguese explorer Vasco da Gama became the first European to sail to India in 1497. His travels opened the trade route between western Europe and the subcontinent. Around this time, some Europeans also came to the subcontinent in hopes of converting the Indian people to Christianity.

By 1757, Great Britain had begun its conquest of the Mughal Empire, taking the subcontinent as part of the British Empire. By 1803, the Mughal rulers had become part of a puppet regime. They retained their titles and the appearance of power, but the British were the ones truly in control of India. By 1876, the British government was outwardly in control of the region, with Queen Victoria adding Empress of India to her official titles.

The British raj, meaning "British rule" in Hindi, united India more than any past empire had. But the British raj also established a deep division between the British officials and most Indian people. British officials lived in large compounds that kept them quite separate from the rest of India. They showed little interest in learning about Indian culture, often dismissing it out of fear and suspicion. Many British people looked down on the Indian people because they were a different race. The British often discriminated against the Indians. Indian soldiers were treated far differently than British military members. The Indians were not allowed to enter British camps or private clubs built for entertainment. They weren't even allowed to handle the most powerful weapons.

The British invested in India only when it served their own purposes. For example, railways were constructed when they became necessary to transport British troops to various regions. When severe droughts made growing food difficult, irrigation systems were an obvious solution. Still, the British did not make this type of infrastructure a priority until they began to worry that Indians could not pay their taxes to the British crown if they did not have enough food.

PRINCELY INDIA

The United Kingdom never gained complete control of the Indian subcontinent. Throughout the British raj, two-fifths of India remained under the control of smaller regimes.[3] The United Kingdom made alliances to work cooperatively with these rulers through numerous treaties. These areas became known as princely India. One of these regions, Hyderabad, was the size of England and Wales.

INDIA'S INDEPENDENCE MOVEMENT

Frustrated by the British raj, many Indians began demanding more involvement in their government. A growing number thought that India should become an independent nation. They formed the Indian National Congress in 1885, a political party that still exists in India. When they presented their ideas about political reform, the British refused to take them seriously. The British insisted that the Indian people were incapable of running their own government. In truth, an independent India would mean great financial loss for the United Kingdom.

When the Indian people began protesting the British raj, some encounters became violent. In 1919, thousands of peaceful protesters gathered in Jallianwala Bagh, an open space in the northwestern city of Amritsar. General Reginald Dyer, the commander of British troops in the area, responded by marching on the crowd. He ordered his soldiers to open fire on the protesters, killing 379 people and injuring about 1,200.[4] Following the horrific incident, the British government forced

THE PATH TO INDIAN CIVIL SERVICE

In 1858, Queen Victoria promised the people of India racial equality of opportunity. Indian people could serve as Indian Civil Service (ICS) officials alongside British people. Civil servants oversaw all government activity in British India's 250 districts. To qualify for one of these spots, however, an Indian had to travel all the way to London to pass a difficult exam, which focused heavily on European subjects. By 1864, only one Indian, Satyendranath Tagore, had passed this test. Although many people asked for exams to be offered in India as well, British officials refused to do so until 1922.

Dyer to retire, but he was never charged with any crime.

The Jallianwala Bagh Massacre led even more Indian people to support the nationalist movement, which sought India's independence from the United Kingdom. One of the movement's most prominent leaders was Mohandas Gandhi, a Hindu lawyer and activist. Born in India, Gandhi had recently returned home from South Africa, where he had protested discrimination against non-white people. Now he worked to convince the British that it was time for the Indian people to rule themselves. Despite further violence from British troops, Gandhi continued to use peaceful methods of protest. He knew that the British could not continue to profit from India without the people's cooperation, so he encouraged nonviolent civil disobedience.

In 1930, Gandhi led his supporters on a 240-mile (386 km) walk to protest the salt tax.[5]

Mohandas Gandhi was the leader of the Indian independence movement.

The British government had made it a crime for an Indian to possess salt that was not purchased from the British monopoly. Gandhi's walk ended at the sea, where he picked up a pinch of salt. He encouraged others to gather their own salt instead of paying the United Kingdom's unfair taxes. British troops once again reacted with violence, but even as they beat many of the protesters with clubs, the Indians remained peaceful. This protest and other protests like it drew the world's attention and pressured the United Kingdom to relinquish its control of India.

TWO NEW NATIONS

Over the next two decades, the United Kingdom gradually transferred governing powers to the Indian people, but both the Hindus and Muslims wanted control of India. The solution on which the British, the Hindus, and the Muslims agreed was dividing India into two new countries. The Hindus would dominate the one called India, while the Muslims would make up a second, new nation called Pakistan. Both countries celebrated their independence from British rule in August 1947. Unfortunately, what should have been a day of festivities after years of struggle as a British colony became a day marked by extreme violence.

The partition of India caused millions of people to leave their homes for the newly established nations. It also led to widespread looting, arson, abductions, murders, and rapes. Revered by both Hindus and Muslims, Gandhi once again tried to help with a peaceful protest. On January 12, 1948, he announced that he would fast until the two groups pledged to make peace with each other. Already in a frail state from fasting, Gandhi was assassinated on January 30, 1948.

The partition of India in 1947 led to mass migrations, which made many people lose their homes.

JAWAHARLAL NEHRU

Jawaharlal Nehru was one of Gandhi's biggest supporters. The two had also been close friends. After joining the Indian National Congress party in 1919, Nehru embraced civil disobedience. He was arrested several times for taking part in peaceful protests. By 1928, the Indian National Congress had named Nehru its president.

As World War II (1939–1945) loomed, Nehru and Gandhi had different opinions about what India's role should be in the conflict. Gandhi wanted to support the United Kingdom. But he thought that India should do so only in a nonviolent manner. Nehru did not think Germany's Nazi government could be stopped in a nonviolent way. He also didn't think India should join the fight unless it could do so as a free country. Despite their differences, Nehru and Gandhi continued to work together for India's independence. When India was named its own nation on August 15, 1947, Nehru became its first prime minister.

INDIA'S RELATIONS WITH PAKISTAN

Despite Hindu and Muslim leaders' promises to Gandhi before his death, peace between India and Pakistan was short lived. Several wars between the two nations have occurred since their creation. The first war began in October 1947 when Pakistan invaded Kashmir. Both countries wanted control of this northernmost region of the subcontinent. The fighting went on for a little over a year with a ceasefire ending the war in early 1949. Conflict between the nations reignited in 1965 when Pakistan again tried to take control of Kashmir. This time, the two nations signed a declaration of peace. But again, it didn't last.

When India and Pakistan became independent nations, Pakistan was split into two parts. The bulk of the new country was located to the west

GANDHI'S ASSASSINATION

Gandhi was walking to a prayer meeting in Delhi when he was killed by a man named Nathuram Godse. The Hindu extremist thought Gandhi was too tolerant of Muslims. Godse bowed to Gandhi in greeting before taking out a pistol and shooting him three times. Although Godse tried to take his own life with a fourth bullet, onlookers restrained him until police arrived. He was sentenced to death after being found guilty of murder.

of India. It was called West Pakistan. A smaller area to the east became East Pakistan. But this part of the country did not want to remain part of Pakistan. In 1971, India joined the war in support of its eastern neighbor. In December, West Pakistan surrendered, and East Pakistan became Bangladesh.

Tension between India and Pakistan continued over the next several decades, particularly over Kashmir. In 2019, India revoked a law it had previously passed that allowed Kashmir some local government control. For example, the law had allowed the area to make laws and fly its own flag. Pakistan responded to these rights being overturned by cutting trade and transportation between the countries. Pakistan also expelled India's ambassador and appealed to the international community.

In 2019, people protested when the Indian government invalidated a law that had given Kashmir limited independence.

CHAPTER **FIVE**

PEOPLE AND CULTURE

In 2021, more than 1.3 billion people lived in India.[1] The country has the second-highest population in the world. China has more people, but India's population is growing faster than China's. In 2022, India was on pace to surpass China as the most populous nation by 2026. More than 50 urban areas in India have populations of over one million people.[2] Mumbai, Delhi, and Bengaluru top the list of these huge cities.

Overpopulation strains the country's resources, worsening problems such as pollution, poverty, and unemployment. Debates about India's population are common in political discussions. Some Indian legislators think that India should impose a law

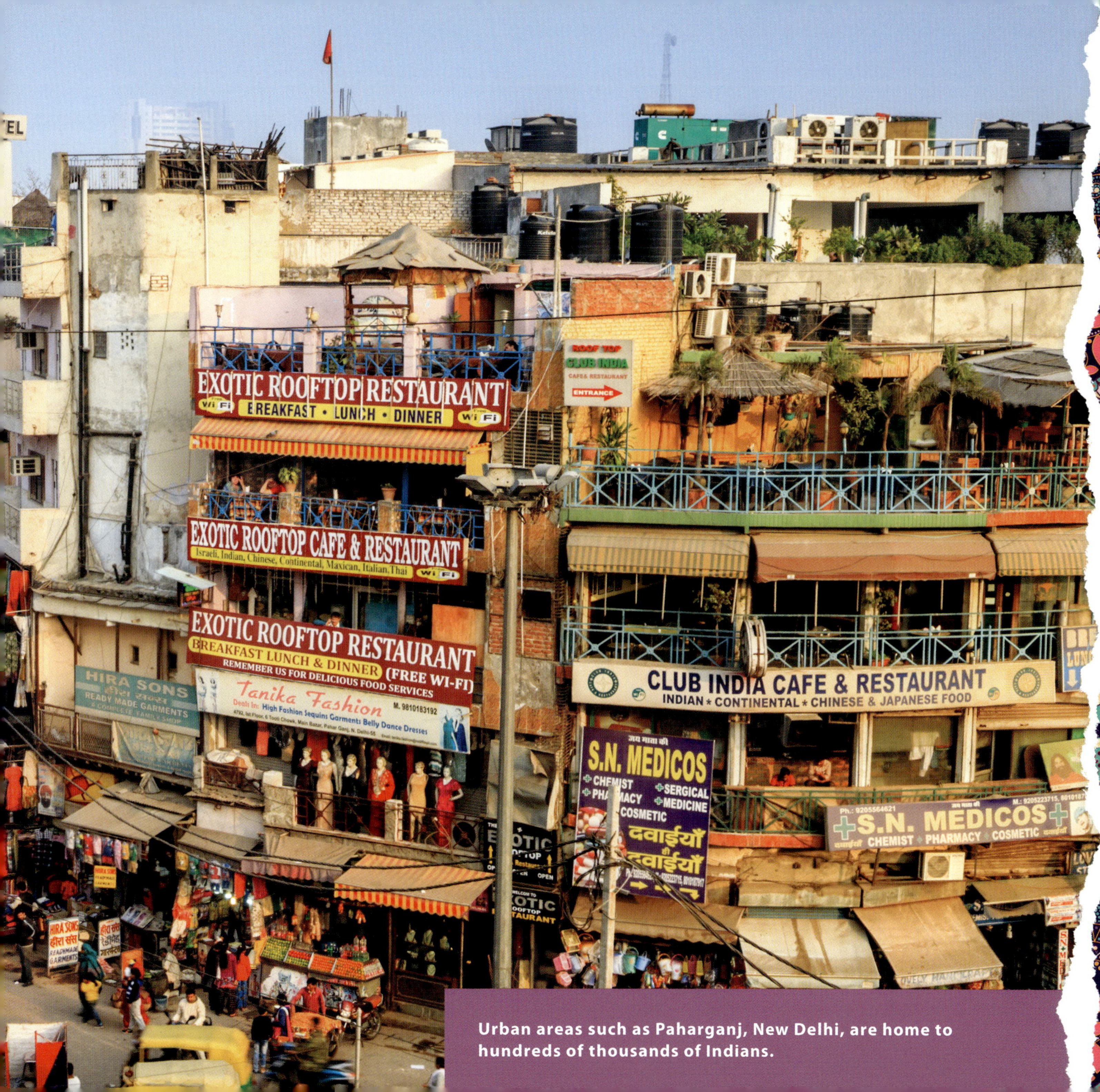

Urban areas such as Paharganj, New Delhi, are home to hundreds of thousands of Indians.

Himachal Pradesh is one of the states of India that is a part of the Hindi Belt.

restricting the number of children that Indian families can have. China has used this approach to slow its population growth. Others think that education can help solve the problem. Although India's population continues to grow, a survey released in 2021 showed that birth rates had begun to slow in recent years. Indian states with the highest literacy levels showed the most slowing of population growth. This is largely because more young women were choosing education over having large families.

ONE NATION, MANY LANGUAGES

India's government officially recognizes 22 languages, but more than 19,500 languages or dialects are spoken in India.[3] Dialects are variations of a particular language. For example, Hindi has 48 official dialects that are spoken in various regions of the country.[4] While some languages are far less common than others, 121 languages are each spoken by at least 10,000 people.[5]

Hindi and English are the two official languages used by the national government. The most common language is Hindi. Most Hindi speakers live in the northern part of the country. Some refer to this area of India as the Hindi Belt for this reason.

English is also spoken in many areas of India. Because it has become such a popular language in other parts of the world, English is often used for conducting business. Some Indians prefer not to use English, however, because they see the language as a symbol of British rule.

About 40 percent of the Indian population speaks Hindi.[7]

Other common languages in India include Bengali, Telugu, and Marathi. Although only 8 percent of the nation speaks Bengali, this totals around 111.7 million people.[6] More than

75 million Indians speak Telugu.[8] Most of them live in southeast India. One distinct characteristic of Telugu is that every word in this language ends in a vowel sound. About 84 million people are native Marathi speakers.[9] This language borrows many words from Arabic, Persian, and its fellow Indian language of Urdu.

The language of Sanskrit is the basis for many other Indian languages. Sometimes called the language of the gods, it was used by scholars in ancient India. Less than 1 percent of Indians still speak Sanskrit.[10] It is now used primarily by Hindu priests during religious ceremonies. However, a few small villages, including Mattur in the southern state of Karnataka, continue to speak it.

A MAP MADE FROM LANGUAGES

India's states were organized based on the languages spoken in the different sections of the country. For instance, Kannada is spoken mainly in the southwestern state of Karnataka. Some states were even named after their most prevalent languages. For example, Punjabi is the most popular language of Punjab. The government of each state is free to select whichever regional language it prefers for its official state language.

FOOD

Indian food is known for being especially flavorful, largely because of its generous use of spices. Cumin, saffron, and turmeric are just a few of the spices used in numerous Indian dishes. Although people outside India often refer to Indian food as a single type of cuisine, food in this nation differs considerably based on the part of India in which it is prepared.

Naan is a type of flatbread that is baked by sticking it to the walls of a tandoor oven.

Meat and vegetable dishes are more common in northern India. Common ingredients used in the north include tomatoes, onions, and yogurt. Many dishes are accompanied with dense, chewy flatbreads such as naan. Northern cooks often bake their breads and other foods in a clay oven called a tandoor. A popular Indian dish called tandoori chicken is named after this oven. Most Indian dishes served in restaurants in other parts of the world originate from northern India.

Food prepared in the southern part of India is mostly vegetarian, although coastal regions often include fish in their meals. Popular ingredients in the south include coconut, green or red chili peppers, and a fruit called tamarind. Rice is used in numerous dishes and in a variety of ways. In addition to being served in its original form, rice is also used for making *idli,* a type of steamed rice cake, and *masala dosa*, a popular type of pancake. Breads aren't as popular in the south except for puri, a fluffy, deep-fried bread.

HINDUISM

Nearly 80 percent of Indian people are Hindu. A little more than 14 percent are Muslim, and slightly more than 2 percent are Christian.[11] Others practice Sikhism, a religion founded in the Punjab region in the 1400s; Buddhism; or other religions. Most Indians respect other religions, but they also spend most of their time with people of their own faiths. Few people marry outside their own religions in India.

CURRY IS NOT AN INDIAN WORD

Outside India, *Indian curry* refers to either a spicy dish made of meat, vegetables, and rice or a blend of hot Indian spices. This word is not used in any Indian language, however. Historians have traced the term to the early 1500s when Portugal captured Goa. The Portuguese likely misunderstood a word the Goans spoke that simply meant "sauce." Years later, some intricate, local Indian dishes were simplified and altered to suit the British colonists' taste. By the end of the 1700s, the British made curry powder, which was a blend of Indian spices. Curry dishes exploded in popularity in Britain, and modern-day curry was born.

Hinduism is the third-largest religion in the world, and it includes many denominations. Although many Indians who practice this religion call themselves Hindus, many do not. The word *Hinduism* was created by British writers in the early 1800s. Many followers of this religion call it the Vedic religion, referring to the Vedas. Other followers call the religion *sanatana dharma*, which means "eternal law."

Hindus believe that souls are immortal. They believe that when people's physical bodies die, their souls go through a process called transmigration, or reincarnation. This means that the soul is reborn into a new body after death. Hindus also believe that a person's next life is determined by karma, the quality of actions from his or her previous life. In Hinduism, the most significant goal is moksha. This is when a soul is freed from the cycle of death and rebirth. Hindus pursue moksha by ritual and action,

Diwali is a festival of lights celebrated by many religions, including Hinduism.

Not all Indians are limited to their castes. B. R. Ambedkar was born into a Dalit family in western India. He later became the law minister of India's government from 1947 to 1951.

knowledge and meditation, or the way of devotion, which includes making pilgrimages and singing hymns.

Hinduism classifies society into four groups called castes. Each caste is said to come from a different part of the god Brahma. Brahmans, who are part of the top caste, include priests and teachers. Coming from Brahma's head, they are considered the greatest intellectuals. Kshatriyas, who include rulers and warriors, are the second group. They are believed to come from Brahma's arms. Next are the Vaishyas, traders who come from Brahma's thighs. This group includes farmers and merchants. The Shudras, who are said to come from the god's feet, perform basic labor. A fifth group called Dalits, or the untouchables, are considered so low in the hierarchy that people belonging to it have no caste. Dalits perform the least-wanted jobs, such as street sweeping and cleaning bathrooms.

In recent years, the caste system's influence has declined, primarily in cities. Social reform movements, urbanization, and secular education have helped deconstruct the system a little and have given more opportunities to the historically disadvantaged. However, caste identities are still common, and people in lower castes still face harsh discrimination.

ARTS

India's long history and varied culture contribute to the nation's diverse arts. Paintings and sculptures from the country are divided into four distinct periods. The ancient period dates from about 3500 BCE until about 1000 CE. Religions such as Hinduism and Buddhism played significant

Bichitr was a Mughal court painter in the mid-1600s. This watercolor and goldleaf piece shows his mastery of art styles.

roles in this work, with sculptures of prominent gods such as Shiva made from stone or bronze. The Mughal Empire lasted from 1526 to 1857 CE. During this period, India's rulers focused largely on opulence. Their art and architecture often included painstaking craftsmanship such as intricate carvings and expensive jewels. The Taj Mahal is a striking example of their appreciation of indulgence. British rule placed a European influence on India's art beginning in 1757. This period lasted until 1947, when India gained independence from the United Kingdom. Since then, Indian art has evolved even more, incorporating traditional and modern elements.

One of the most popular forms of art in India is Madhubani painting. This art form is known for its vibrant colors, geometric patterns, and double-lined borders. It was first mentioned in the *Ramayana*, a widely revered ancient Hindu text. While preparing for his daughter Sita's

MINI **BIO**

PRIYANKA CHOPRA

Priyanka Chopra was born in Jamshedpur, India, on July 18, 1982. She is a famous model and actress known far beyond the nation's borders. While she was still in high school, Chopra entered and won the Miss India pageant. She later competed and won the Miss World pageant in 2000. Following her reign as Miss World, Chopra pursued a career as a Bollywood actress. Her first big hit was a romantic comedy called *Mujhse Shaadi Karogi*.

By 2014, Chopra was given more serious roles in film, including the role of female boxer Mary Kom. *Mary Kom* was the first Hindi film ever included in the first night of the Toronto International Film Festival. The following year, Chopra accepted the lead role in the television series *Quantico*. She was the first Indian woman to star in a US television drama series.

Chopra announced in 2018 that she was engaged to American singer and actor Nick Jonas. The couple married in December with an extravagant wedding at a palace in Jodhpur, India. They welcomed their first child in January 2022.

Priyanka Chopra is an internationally famous actress.

wedding, King Janaka asked his painters to create Madhubani paintings for the event. Madhubani painting has deep roots in the Mithila region of Bihar. Contemporary Madhubani paintings are often featured at weddings and festivals in the region.

Indian music is as varied as the country's graphic arts. Bhangra music began in the state of Punjab with field workers singing songs to the beat of a dhol drum. Today this popular genre has become a fusion of traditional Indian folk music and Western sounds. Modern synthesizers now add to the beat. This music can be heard in many bhangra clubs.

Dandiya music is especially popular in Gujrat, but it is also enjoyed throughout the rest of India. Large groups gather to perform the Dandiya Raas dance, also called the stick dance. The nickname comes from the sticks the dancers carry, which they strike together to the beat. Both the music and the dance are found at Navratri festivals. These festivals honor the goddess Durga each autumn.

Music is a major part of Bollywood films. Singing and choreographed dancing are woven into the storylines. Even in more serious films, music plays in the background as the stories unfold. Most Bollywood films have soundtracks that fans can buy. In recent years, some Bollywood producers have used the music's popularity to their advantage. They often release a movie's soundtrack before the film premieres, hoping it will draw more people to movie showings later.

SPORTS

Sports are a huge part of modern Indian culture. The most popular by far is cricket. This game, which is similar to baseball, was introduced to India by British sailors in the 1700s.

NEW LIFE FOR AN OLD GAME

Indians have been playing chess for thousands of years, but interest in the game has risen dramatically since Viswanathan Anand became a world champion in 2000. The grandmaster, who went on to win four more world championships, has inspired many people in the nation to take up the board game. He is revered throughout India as a national hero.

Some professional cricket players, such as Virat Kohli and Sachin Tendulkar, are even more famous in India than the most popular Bollywood actors.

Soccer is another popular sport in India. Although India's national soccer team has not made much of a name for itself at the international level, it is the second-most-watched sport in the country. Other games that rank among Indian fans' top sports include field hockey, badminton, and tennis.

CHAPTER **SIX**

POLITICS

India's government is a federal parliamentary republic similar to the United Kingdom's government system. In a parliamentary republic, Indian citizens elect many of their representatives to make laws and decisions for the country. Although individual voters are not involved in each decision the government makes, the people have the power to elect representatives who most closely align with their political values. The government is divided into three branches: the executive branch, the legislative branch, and the judicial branch. These branches have different responsibilities to check each other's power.

India's executive government branch includes the president, vice president, and council of ministers.

Vidhana Soudha is a state legislative building in Bengaluru, India.

Ram Nath Kovind became India's president in 2017.

They are all led by the nation's prime minister. The prime minister is appointed by the president after being elected by members of the Lok Sabha, which is the lower house of India's parliament. The council of ministers are then appointed by the prime minister. The president is elected by an electoral college, which consists of both members of Parliament and members of the states' legislative assemblies. All members pledge to support the candidate who wins the popular vote. The vice president is also elected by an electoral college, but this one consists only of parliamentary members. The prime minister and the president are both elected for five years, and then they can run for additional terms.

Ram Nath Kovind became president of India in 2017. Although he heads the country, his role is largely ceremonial. Some people compare the job of the president to that of a monarch in the Netherlands, the United Kingdom, or Spain.

India's president has very little political control. The president can, however, offer advice and warnings to the ministers who do make most of the decisions.

Narendra Modi became India's prime minister in 2014. As the top leader of the nation, he is in charge of several ministries and departments. He must also communicate to the president all decisions made by the Council of Ministers.

The legislative branch is India's Parliament. It is made up of two houses. The upper house is called the Rajya Sabha. Most of its members are voted into office by the state legislatures. The president appoints 12 members to represent art, literature, science, and social services. India's president also heads this branch of the government, but the role is largely ceremonial. The prime minister heads the lower house, the Lok Sabha. Either house can propose most new legislation. Both houses must vote in favor of a bill for it to become law. The exception are bills that relate to the nation's finances, which can be introduced only by the Lok Sabha.

The Rajya Sabha consists of up to 250 members. The Lok Sabha can have up to 530 members from the states and an additional 20 members from union territories.

The judicial branch includes India's Supreme Court, the highest court in the nation. It is made up of 34 judges, one of whom serves as the chief justice. This court hears a wide range of cases. Some involve the interpretation of the nation's constitution, federal disputes, disputes between states, and appeals from cases already heard by lower courts. The Supreme Court has the final say in all these matters.

THE WORLD'S LONGEST CONSTITUTION

At 145,000 words, India's constitution is the longest of any country in the world—and not just by a little. The document is more than 32 times the length of the US Constitution. The original document, which India adopted in 1950, contained 395 articles. Since then, amendments have increased this total to 448, with more likely to be added in the future. Two handwritten copies of this lengthy document are on display in the library of India's Parliament House. One is in Hindi, and the other is in English.

MAJOR POLITICAL PARTIES

India has a multiparty system, which includes a long list of political parties. The Election Commission of India classifies each party into a national, state, or regional level. Only the most successful parties are granted status at the national level. This can be done one of three ways. The first is by winning at least 2 percent of seats in the Lok Sabha, with the winning candidates representing at least three different states. Another way is by winning at least 6 percent of the vote in the country's national election, as well as four Lok Sabha seats. The third way is by becoming a state-level party in at least four states. The qualification process at the state level is similar.

Although regional parties are considerably smaller than state and national parties, they sometimes have a tremendous impact on Indian politics. Unlike state and national parties, regional parties do not need to win a certain number of seats or percentage of the vote. Many of these

Mayawati Kumari was a major figure of the Bahujan Samaj Party. She was named the party's president in 2003.

smaller parties make alliances with one another, which give them more power than they would have individually.

Only a handful of parties have drawn large enough followings to make a significant impact on the Indian government at the national level. Those with the largest presence include the Bahujan Samaj Party, the Communist Party of India, Communist Party of India Marxist, and the Nationalist

Congress Party. The top two parties are the Bharatiya Janata Party (BJP) and the Indian National Congress (INC).

The BJP was formed in 1980. Its name means "the Indian people's party." The BJP is considered a right-wing party, meaning it supports conservative values. It is also a pro-Hindu party. Dating to the British raj, the INC is the oldest of all India's political parties. Following India's independence, the INC took a liberal approach to politics, meaning it supports more progressive values. This party supports equal rights regardless of caste.

POLITICAL SYMBOLS

About three weeks before India officially gained its independence from the United Kingdom in 1947, the Constituent Assembly adopted its flag, an important symbol of India's new status as a free country. This assembly was put in place a year earlier to create India's constitution. Indians have nicknamed the flag the Tricolor, referring to the three colors that make up its background. Each color has significance. The top stripe is saffron, a reddish-orange color, which represents the country's courage and strength. The white middle

THE ASHOKA CHAKRA

The wheel at the center of India's flag is called the Ashoka Chakra. Some Indians say the spokes symbolize the 24 Rishis of the Himalayas. According to Hinduism, these were the seers who recorded the religion's ancient scriptures. Others say the spokes symbolize the 24 hours in a day and that the chakra represents the movement of time. They think the chakra tells the Indian people not to resist change and to keep moving forward.

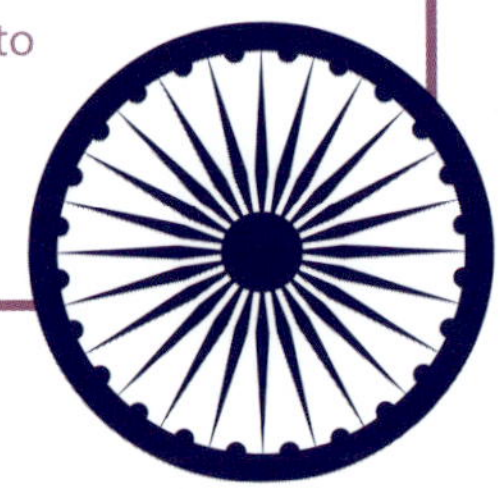

MINI **BIO**

INDIRA GANDHI

Indira Gandhi was the first female prime minister of India. Born in 1917 in Prayagraj, Indira grew up as India struggled for independence. After attending India's Visva-Bharati University and the University of Oxford in England, Indira joined the Indian National Congress (INC) in 1938. A few years later, she married fellow INC member Feroze Gandhi. In 1959, she became the party's president.

After serving in the Rajya Sabha and as minister of information and broadcasting, she became India's prime minister in 1966. While in office, she played a key role in helping East Pakistan gain its own independence in 1971. Gandhi was the first world leader to acknowledge the new nation as Bangladesh. Gandhi was reelected three times, but her final term as India's prime minister was cut short in 1984 when she was assassinated by two of her own bodyguards.

Although they share a last name, Indira Gandhi was not related to Mohandas Gandhi.

Many Indians raise their flags during Republic Day, which commemorates India's independence and the adoption of its constitution in 1950.

stripe symbolizes peace and truth. A dark blue wheel called the Ashoka Chakra appears in the center of this white band. It represents the movement of life. The bottom green stripe stands for fertility and growth.

For many years, Indian citizens were allowed to fly the country's flag only on national holidays, but this changed in 2002. The government changed the flag code so the people could raise flags over their homes or workplaces on any day of the year, providing they followed the rules and regulations for its respectful display. These include flying the flag only between sunrise and sunset and never flying another flag, such as a state flag, higher than the Indian flag.

Another celebrated symbol of India is its national anthem, "Jana Gana Mana." The song was written by the Nobel laureate Rabindranath Tagore. Although the song became the country's national anthem in 1950, it was first sung publicly in 1911 at a meeting of the INC by Tagore himself. Part of the song's universal appeal is that Tagore used lyrics that were familiar to everyone in India who heard them. Nearly all the nouns in the anthem are common to all the major languages of the nation.

ONE SONG, TWO VERSIONS

The full version of "Jana Gana Mana" has five stanzas. Because it takes a long time to sing all of them, a much shorter version of the national anthem is sometimes played at special events in the country. This version consists only of the first and last lines of the song.

INDIA'S MILITARY

India's military consists of the Indian Army, the Indian Navy, and the Indian Air Force. Together, they make up the second-largest military with active-duty members in the world.[1] Only China has more active-duty members. Led by the chief of army staff in New Delhi, the Indian Army includes six field armies and one training command. Each of these groups has its own lieutenant general to command it. This structure of India's armed forces has existed since the nation gained independence from the United Kingdom.

The Indian Army is an all-volunteer force, and it's the world's largest volunteer army.

An early version of the Indian Navy was established in the 1800s when the East India Company wanted a maritime presence in the region. This group evolved into the Royal Indian Navy in 1934. The modern Indian Navy is led by the chief of the naval staff in New Delhi. This admiral commands three groups—two in the Arabian Sea and one in the Bay of Bengal.

The Indian Navy has approximately 57,240 sailors.[2] The Indian Air Force has more than 170,000 members. The Indian Army has about three million members.[3]

The Indian Air Force was formed in 1932 under British control. In 1954, its command transferred to its first Indian chief of air staff, Air Marshal Subroto Mukerjee. He was one of the founding members of the force.

CHAPTER **SEVEN**

ECONOMICS

India's economy is the fourth-largest in the world.[1] Its biggest industries include agriculture, services, and manufacturing. Rice, spices, and wheat are among the top foods produced in the country. India grows many of the world's fruits and vegetables. The country's top fruit exports include bananas, mangoes, and pomegranates. Onions, potatoes, and tomatoes top the list of exported vegetables. India also grows large crops of guavas, papayas, cabbages, and cauliflower.

About 60 percent of the workforce in India was employed in the agriculture sector in 2020.[2]

India is a huge contributor to the global economy. For example, the driverless metro trains used in Sydney, Australia, were assembled in Andhra Pradesh, India.

India is the world's largest producer of milk. With its huge Hindu population, the country also consumes more milk than any other. Several Hindu gods and goddesses are associated with cows, and Hindus use milk in many of their religious rituals. Indians also use milk in many foods and drinks—from sweets to tea. Dairy farms across the country produce enough milk to meet India's demand for 171 million tons (155 million metric tons) of milk each year.[3]

THE SPICE TRADE

India is the largest producer, consumer, and exporter of spices. The nation produces about half the spices exported around the world.[6] Australia, Canada, and the United States are among the top importers of these products. These spices include cumin, ginger, and turmeric. India is known for the quality of its spices. Their aroma, texture, and taste often place them high above spices produced elsewhere.

THE SERVICE INDUSTRY

A third of Indian people work in the service sector. This industry includes hotels, restaurants, transportation, banking and finance, and other business services. Travel and tourism income in India totaled more than $194 billion in 2019.[4] Much of the country's revenue from this industry comes from within India, with people traveling from one region to another, but many foreign visitors also visit the country. In 2018, more than 10.5 million tourists made the trip from outside the country.[5]

Information technology (IT) services have become an especially important part of India's service industry, with many English-speaking countries outsourcing their IT departments to India because of the large percentage of Indians who are both well-educated in technology and fluent in English. American Express, Ford, and Microsoft are just a few of the world's top companies that have moved their IT departments to India. Because the cost of labor is much lower in India than in many other countries, companies often end up saving large amounts of money by making this type of move.

NATURAL RESOURCES AND MANUFACTURING

India's abundant natural resources make manufacturing a big part of the country's economy. One of India's most successful manufacturing companies is Hindalco Industries. It is the world's largest aluminum rolling company. Rolling is a process that takes a large slab of metal and turns it into a more flexible material, which is used by a variety of other companies. For example, food and beverage companies use aluminum to make foil, cans, and other types of containers. Architectural companies use it to make roofing, siding, and gutters.

Another leading manufacturer in India is Tata Steel, which was established in 1907. The company produces steel that is used in a huge range of industries including auto manufacturing, construction, and aerospace. In addition to its

A NEW KIND OF INDEPENDENCE

In August 2021, India's prime minister, Narendra Modi, pledged that the nation would become energy independent by the one-hundredth anniversary of its independence. If his pledge proves to be accurate, it means that the nation will consume no energy produced by other countries by 2047.

headquarters and plants in India, Tata Steel also has factories in numerous other countries around the world.

Coal is another one of India's most abundant natural resources. The country is estimated to have 100 billion short tons (91 billion metric tons) of coal reserves.[7] In addition to providing the nation with energy, coal also provides many people with jobs. More than four million Indian people are employed in the coal sector.[8] One of the biggest companies, Coal India, has 84 mining complexes in eight different states. Many global leaders think that India should reduce its reliance on coal because burning it releases harmful chemicals into the environment. But India is unlikely to give up coal anytime soon. The nation greatly depends on its use.

HONORING GANDHI

Images of Mohandas Gandhi have appeared on all Indian banknotes since 1996, but this was not the first time the beloved leader was featured on the nation's currency. India released a commemorative 100-rupee banknote bearing Gandhi's image on what would have been his one-hundredth birthday in 1969. A 500-rupee banknote was also added in 1987, nearly a decade before the full series of denominations with his image was released.

INDIA'S CURRENCY

India's rupee is both a modern form of currency and a link to India's ancient past. Early forms of the currency have been traced to the 500s BCE. The word *rupee* comes from the Sanskrit word *rupya*, which means "silver." India was one of the first regions of the world to mint coins.

Sher Shah Suri, founder of India's Suri empire, issued the rupiya coin in the mid-1500s. It was a precursor of the rupee. When the British East India Company began doing business in India in the 1600s, the British tried to convert the region to its currency, the pound sterling, but India resisted. The Indian people continued using the rupiya in trade. The British accepted so much of the coin that they even introduced it to other British colonies. When India came under the control of the United Kingdom, the nation put an image of its monarch on the rupiya. However, after 1857, the United Kingdom made the rupee the official form of currency of India.

Today people in different regions of India call the rupee by different names, including rupaya, roopayi, rubai, and ropa. In addition to the single rupee, coins also come in denominations of 2 and 5 rupees. Banknotes are issued in denominations of 5, 10, 20, 50, 100, 500, and 1,000 rupees.

The rupee is India's official currency.

Each rupee is equivalent to 100 paise. A single unit of this currency is called a paisa. India added the paisa to its economy in 1957 so that the rupee could be divided into smaller amounts, similar to how the US dollar is divided into cents.

TRANSPORTATION AND INFRASTRUCTURE

India's roads and railways are among the most heavily traveled in the world. Companies use them to transport their goods through the nation, and people rely on them for traveling to and from work each day, as well as exploring the country for recreation. Large national highways connect the various regions of India to one another. National Highway 44 is one of the most used. Starting in the northern city of Srinagar, it spans 2,555 miles (4,112 km) to the southern town of Kanniyakumari. It connects 11 states and 30 of the country's important cities. Running east to west, National Highway 27 is nearly 2,556 miles (4,113 km) long.[9] Although it runs through only seven states, this highway connects 47 cities.

In addition to commercial trucks and passenger vehicles, city buses are a common sight on India's roads. They are among the most common modes of transportation in urban areas, as the inexpensive fares are affordable for many. Sightseeing buses are popular among tourists in India, but many tourists prefer the comfort of traveling by train. All the railways in India are owned and operated by the government. The Mountain

The Nilgiri Mountain Railway in Tamil Nadu reaches an elevation of 7,228 feet (2,203 m).[10]

India's railway network is the fourth-largest in the world. Its total route length is 42,225 miles (67,956 km).

Railways, which transport passengers through the hills and foothills of three different mountain ranges, were collectively named a UNESCO World Heritage site in 2008. This has made these sections of India's railways among the most traveled in the world.

Much of India's infrastructure needs improvement. India's large population makes the upkeep of roads and bridges a continual concern. The nation's roadways carry 65 percent of India's freight and 90 percent of its passenger traffic each day.[11] That adds up to a lot of wear and tear on India's roads. In September 2021, the government granted $980.9 million for road safety projects in 14 states. These states have the most total road fatalities in the country.[12]

CHAPTER **EIGHT**

INDIA TODAY

The family unit is a focal point of modern life in India. Most households include more than one generation, with parents, children, and grandchildren sharing homes. Many marriages are arranged by elder family members. In these cases, spouses are typically chosen based on caste, religion, and wealth. However, some young adults decide to marry for love instead. After a couple marries, it is common for them to reside with the groom's family.

At just 1.1 percent, the divorce rate in India is the lowest in the world.[1] Some people might assume that this means marriages in the country are happier than elsewhere in the world. But this isn't necessarily

Many Indians believe in the value of family.

the case. The number of married people who are separated in India is three times higher than the number of people who are legally divorced.[2] A more likely reason for the low divorce rate is that divorce still has a huge stigma. Many people in India view divorce as a sign of failure.

India is a patriarchal society, which means men occupy most leadership positions at home and in the workplace. Men are expected to earn money, while women are expected to care for their children and homes. The oldest male in a household is usually the head of the family, the person who has the final say in most family matters. Unmarried women are expected to obey their fathers, while married women give their husbands this same obedience. This type of toxic patriarchy and gender bias has contributed to numerous accounts of intentionally neglected girls and exploited women.

In 2020, only about 19 percent of women were in the workforce in India.[3]

When a woman marries, her family presents her husband's family with a dowry. Although giving or receiving a dowry has been illegal in India since 1961, it is still a common practice. The exact value of a dowry differs based on the family's caste and economic status. In rural areas, a dowry might include livestock. For wealthier families, a dowry may include expensive jewelry or real estate. Many Indians define a dowry as a gift of gratitude for welcoming the bride into her new family. But in some instances, a dowry has also become a negotiating factor in an arranged marriage to build wealth.

INDIA'S EDUCATIONAL SYSTEM

Under Indian law, all children are required to start primary school at age six. However, many parents send their children to preschool and kindergarten at an earlier age to prepare them for their lower primary education. Montessori schools, which focus on hands-on learning activities, are an especially popular preschool choice in the country. Public schools, which are run by the government, are free, but many of these schools get low funding. Some parents think private schools are better, but many Indian families cannot afford the tuition. Spots in these schools are also limited, so academic competition for them is high.

Primary school includes grades one through five. All instruction is provided in the language of the geographical region. By grade three, students begin learning English as a second language. After primary school, students move to middle school, where they continue until they complete grade eight. Secondary school begins at grade nine. Education continues to be free at public schools at this level. However, more students attend private schools by this point if possible. Beginning in grade nine, students start learning a third language of their choice. They study math, science and technology, social sciences, art, and physical education. Many students who do not plan on going to college start studying a vocation.

Indian schools focus strongly on academics. Tests are routine events, and much of learning consists of memorization. Subjects that encourage creative thinking are not commonly offered, and extracurricular activities are rare. The goal of school is to learn academic subjects so that students can continue their education and make a good living in the future. For this reason,

In India, uniforms are mandatory in public and private schools.

students shift their educational focus toward their individual goals starting in grade 11. This is when most young people choose their career paths.

Students who choose to go to college can earn a bachelor's degree in three years in most majors. Medicine and engineering programs last longer. Students can also attend college for one additional year for a graduate degree. Among the most prestigious universities in India are the Indian Institute of Technology Bombay in Mumbai, the Indian Institute of Science in Bengaluru, and the University of Delhi.

GAMES INDIAN KIDS ENJOY

When they aren't in school, Indian children love to play games, as do many adults. One of the most popular board games in the country is called pachisi. The game was called Parcheesi when it came to the United States in the late 1800s, but it was invented in India much earlier, around 500 BCE. Pachisi is named after the Hindi word *pachis*, which means twenty-five. This is the highest score a pachisi player can throw using cowry shells. People play the game on a board in the shape of a cross. In the middle of the cross is a large square called the Charkoni. Two to four players play with the goal of bringing all their pieces to the Charkoni.

Another popular game is called kanche. The game is played with marbles. Several variations of the game exist, but most are based on players taking turns shooting their marbles at other

Some modern pachisi games use dice instead of cowry shells.

marbles in the game. If players knock another player's marbles outside a circle, they can win and keep those marbles. The winner is the person with the most marbles at the end of the game.

Other children's games in India are more physical. One is a game called gilli danda, which is like cricket with a twist. Players use a long stick called a danda and a short stick called a gilli, which has tapered ends. They use the danda to flip the gilli in the air, and then they hit it as far as they can. If a player on the opposing team catches the gilli while it is in the air, the hitter's turn is over. If no one catches it, the hitter's score is equal to the number of danda lengths the gilli travels. Knocking the gilli into the air and hitting it before it falls to the ground requires practice. People with good hand-eye coordination do well at this game.

A LESSON IN KARMA

One of the most popular board games in India goes by many names. Among them is Gyan Chaupar, which means "the game of knowledge." Some historians say the game was invented by the ancient Indian poet Sant Dnyaneshwar. The game's original purpose was to teach children about karma. Good deeds afford players the opportunity to climb ladders, while poor choices send them sliding down snakes. The game eventually spread to other countries, where it is commonly known as Snakes and Ladders or Chutes and Ladders.

MODERN CHALLENGES

One of the biggest problems in India is poverty. In 2020, about 60 percent of Indians lived below the poverty line.[4] The poverty line marks the minimum income needed to provide a person with basic needs such as food, shelter, and clothing. Most people under the poverty line live in the nation's rural villages. The states that struggle with poverty the most are Madhya Pradesh, Uttar Pradesh, Bihar, Chhattisgarh, and Jharkhand.

India also struggles with rampant pollution. Massive air pollution has resulted from India's heavy traffic, numerous industrial plants, and the burning of fossil fuels for power. Smog is visible in many cities. All the pollutants affect people's health, leading to heart and lung diseases, immune system issues, and even cognitive problems. In the most polluted areas, children often cough if they play too vigorously outdoors. Some people say they feel tired when they first get up in the morning due to the poor air quality.

Much of the water in India is also heavily polluted. One of the most polluted waterways is the Ganges. Industry is partially to blame for this problem, as many businesses have been built along the river. Chemical plants, textile mills, and even slaughterhouses dump waste from their operations into the river. Human waste is also a major culprit. More than 792,000 gallons (3 million L) of raw sewage are emptied into the Ganges daily.[5]

COVID-19 IN INDIA

When the COVID-19 pandemic began in early 2020, India took major safety measures. Nearly all businesses, schools, and other public spaces closed to prevent the virus from spreading. The strategy worked well for the first year, but the number of cases began rising again. In May 2021, India had the most COVID-19 cases in the world and a daily average of more than 4,000 deaths.[6] In mid-2022, the country's total death count from the disease was 524,903.[7] A massive vaccination effort made a substantial difference. By March 2022, India had vaccinated more than 765 million adults and about 28 million teenagers between ages 15 and 18.[8] Cases dropped quickly. After two years, India finally started reopening life.

Although the Yamuna River is one of India's holiest rivers, it is also one of India's most polluted rivers.

YOGA

Many Indians practice yoga daily. This series of stretches and postures meant to bring the body and the mind into harmony originated in India thousands of years ago. It existed even before most current religions. The word *yoga* comes from the Sanskrit word *yuj*, which means "to unite." Now practiced in many other places in the world, yoga is believed to bring spiritual balance into the lives of people who practice it. It can also be great exercise. The Hindu god Shiva is said to have been the very first yogi. This title is given to those considered experts in yoga.

Only about half of the sewage goes through treatment facilities that remove toxic contaminants.

As India's waterways are being polluted, the country is experiencing another kind of water crisis. Extreme weather patterns have led to continual droughts in the country, which make fresh water harder to find, particularly in rural areas. In the most remote regions, people must walk miles to collect water for drinking, cooking, and bathing. Most often, women are expected to perform this strenuous task, which is getting more and more difficult in drier places. Climate change, which is made worse by industrial pollution, intensifies the extreme weather causing India's water scarcity. If nothing is done to slow climate change, water will become even harder to find in the future.

Despites its many challenges, India remains one of the most beautiful and culturally rich countries in the world. Its religions, cuisine, and history have had a profound impact on much of the world. India is a nation filled with wonders for all who visit or call it home.

ESSENTIAL **FACTS**

OFFICIAL NAME: REPUBLIC OF INDIA

GEOGRAPHY

Area: 1,269,219 square miles (3,287,263 sq km)

Highest Elevation: Kanchenjunga at 28,169 feet (8,586 m)

Lowest Elevation: Indian Ocean at 0 feet (0 m)

PEOPLE

Population: 1.39 billion (2022 est.)

Most Populous City: New Delhi (32.2 million)

Ethnic Groups: Indo-Aryan, Dravidian, other

Religions: Hinduism, Islam, Christianity, Sikhism, Buddhism

GOVERNMENT

Type of Government: Federal parliamentary republic

Capital: New Delhi

Head of State: President

Head of Government: Prime minister

Legislature: Bicameral, with the Rajya Sabha and Lok Sabha

ECONOMY

Currency: Indian rupee

Major Industries: Agriculture, service, manufacturing

Natural Resources: Coal, antimony, iron ore, lead, manganese, mica, bauxite, rare earth elements, titanium ore, chromite, natural gas, diamonds, petroleum, limestone, farmable land

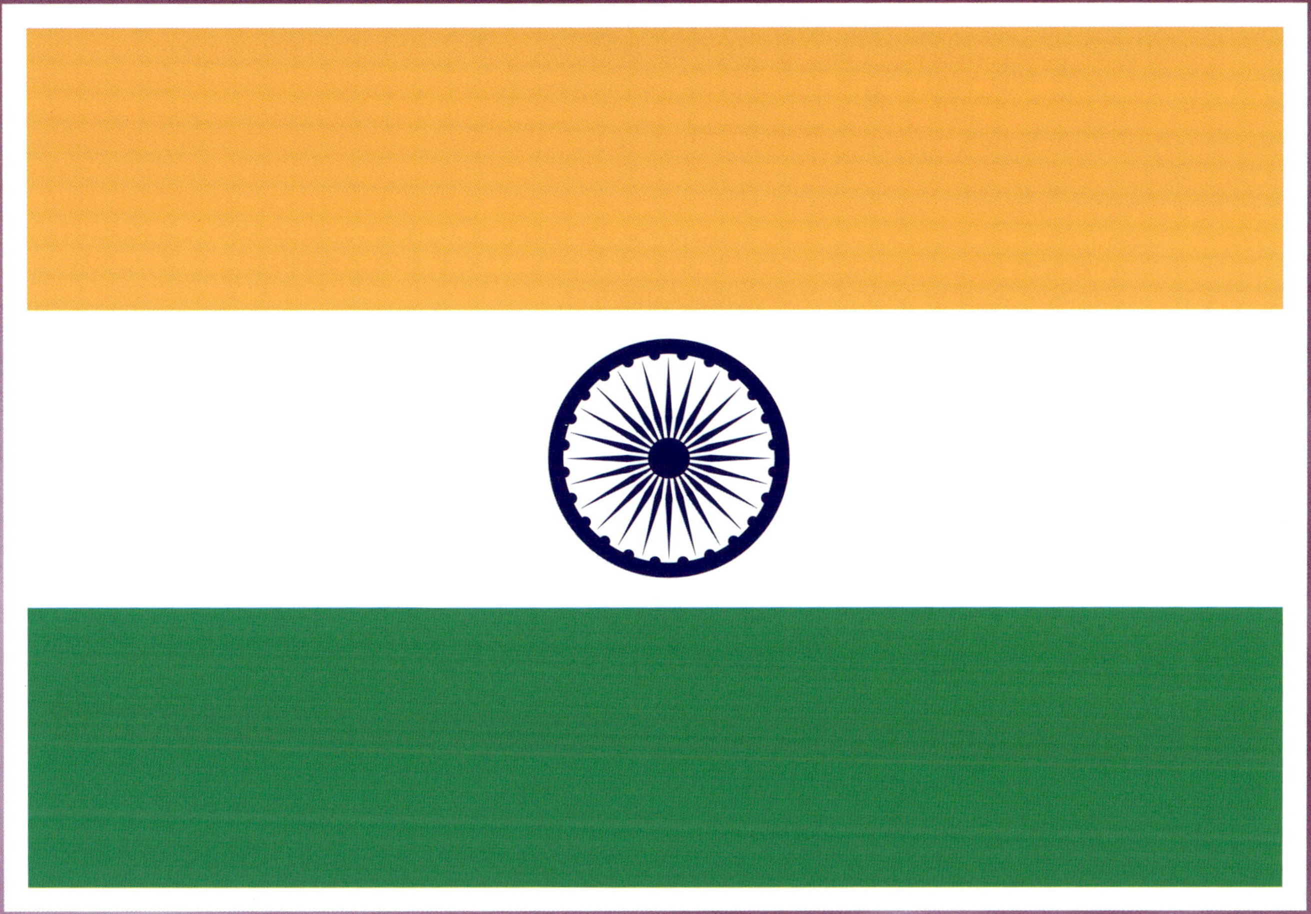

NATIONAL SYMBOLS

National Anthem: "Jana Gana Mana" ("Thou Art the Ruler of All Minds")

National Bird: Indian peacock

National Animal: Bengal tiger

GLOSSARY

AEROSPACE
The manufacturing industry that specializes in aircraft and spacecraft.

CIVIL DISOBEDIENCE
The act of refusing to obey certain laws in hopes of changing them.

COGNITIVE
Related to the act or process of thinking, remembering, or learning.

DECIDUOUS
A type of tree that sheds its leaves annually.

DIALECT
A regional variety of a language with distinct vocabulary, grammar, and accent.

DOWRY
An amount of money or valuable goods brought by the bride's family to the groom's family on the day of marriage.

INFRASTRUCTURE
The physical structures, such as roads, railways, and power plants, that make it possible for a city or nation to function.

ITINERARY
A list of planned activities.

LAUREATE
A person who is honored with an award.

MANGROVE
A shrub or tree with tangled roots that grows near the coast in tropical swamps that flood at high tide.

MAUSOLEUM
A structure built to house one or more tombs.

PATRIARCHAL
Characteristic of a system of society or government in which men are dominant.

PUPPET REGIME
A government with symbolic positions of authority that hold little to no actual power.

STIGMA
A set of negative and often unfair beliefs that a society or group of people has about something.

ADDITIONAL **RESOURCES**

SELECTED BIBLIOGRAPHY

"India." *CIA World Factbook*, 11 Apr. 2022, cia.gov. Accessed 14 Apr. 2022.

"Mauryan Empire." *National Geographic*, 19 Aug. 2020, nationalgeographic.org. Accessed 14 Apr. 2022.

"Soul of India: Timeline." *PBS*, 19 Dec. 2008, pbs.org. Accessed 14 Apr. 2022.

FURTHER READINGS

Buckey, A. W. *Understanding Buddhism*. Abdo, 2019.

Gilmour, David. *The British in India: A Social History of the Raj*. Farrar, Straus and Giroux, 2018.

Nardo, Don. *Understanding Hinduism*. ReferencePoint, 2019.

ONLINE RESOURCES

Booklinks NONFICTION NETWORK
FREE! ONLINE NONFICTION RESOURCES

To learn more about India, please visit **abdobooklinks.com** or scan this QR code. These links are routinely monitored and updated to provide the most current information available.

MORE INFORMATION

For more information on this subject, contact or visit the following organizations:

The Hindu
Kasturi Buildings, 859&860, Anna Salai
Chennai 600002
thehindu.com
The Hindu is India's renowned English-language daily newspaper. It is known for its accurate coverage of breaking news and news about politics, sports, business, and arts and entertainment.

The Indian Museum
27, Jawaharlal Nehru Road, Park St.
Kolkata, West Bengal 700016
indianmuseumkolkata.org
Founded in 1814, the Indian Museum is the largest and oldest museum in India. The museum has a rare collection of Mughal paintings, mummies, antiques, and more.

Ministry of Tourism
Room No.119, Transport Bhawan, 1, Sansad Marg
New Delhi, Delhi 110001
tourism.gov.in
The Ministry of Tourism is the government agency in charge of developing tourism in India. It also promotes and markets tourism overseas.

SOURCE **NOTES**

CHAPTER 1. A TOUR OF INDIA

1. "Some Interesting Facts You Didn't Know about Taj Mahal." *Tour My India*, 19 Dec. 2020, tourmyindia.com. Accessed 10 Mar. 2022.
2. "Agra Fort." *Encyclopedia Britannica*, n.d., britannica.com. Accessed 10 Mar. 2022.
3. "Taj Mahal." *Encyclopedia Britannica*, n.d., britannica.com. Accessed 10 Mar. 2022.
4. "What Is Bollywood? A Brief History of Bollywood Films." *Master Class*, 25 Feb. 2022, masterclass.com. Accessed 13 Mar. 2022.
5. "National Parks." *Wildlife Institute of India*, 31 May 2022, wii.gov.in. Accessed 13 Mar. 2022.
6. Joe Hartley. "Indian Languages: A Useful Guide to All the Languages Spoken in India." *Berlitz*, 31 Oct. 2021, berlitz.com. Accessed 13 Mar. 2022.

CHAPTER 2. GEOGRAPHY

1. "Largest Countries in the World." *Worldometer*, n.d., worldometers.info. Accessed 10 Mar. 2022.
2. "India." *Encyclopedia Britannica*, 15 June 2022, britannica.com. Accessed 10 Mar. 2022.
3. "Rajasthan." *Encyclopedia Britannica*, n.d., britannica.com. Accessed 13 Mar. 2022.
4. "Goa." *Encyclopedia Britannica*, n.d., britannica.com. Accessed 13 Mar. 2022.
5. "Kanchenjunga." *Encyclopedia Britannica*, 2 Dec. 2019, britannica.com. Accessed 13 Mar. 2022.
6. "List of Indian States by Area." *Statistics Times*, 7 July 2020, statisticstimes.com. Accessed 13 Mar. 2022.
7. Sharell Cook. "12 Major Mountain Ranges in India." *Tripsavvy*, 9 Nov. 2019, tripsavvy.com. Accessed 13 Mar. 2022.
8. Sharell Cook, "12 Major Mountain Ranges in India."
9. Parth Saikia. "Purvanchal Range of Northeast India." *North East India Info*, 25 Dec. 2020, northeastindiageography.blogspot.com. Accessed 15 Mar. 2022.
10. "Best Time to Visit Kanchenjunga." *A Complete Guide for Trekking in Nepal*, 5 Oct. 2020, radianttreks.com. Accessed 15 Mar. 2022.
11. "Thar Desert." *Encyclopedia Britannica*, n.d., britannica.com. Accessed 15 Mar. 2022.
12. "Thar Desert," *Encyclopedia Britannica*.
13. Resham Sengar. "Do You Know the Epic Story about the Formation of Thar Desert?" *Times Travel*, 16 Mar. 2019, timesofindia.indiatimes.com. Accessed 15 Mar. 2022.
14. Ananda Banerjee. "Subdari Trees in Sundarban Delta Are Dying a Slow Death. Is Anyone Listening?" *Outlook*, 4 June 2020, outlookindia.com. Accessed 20 Mar. 2022.
15. Amanda Briney. "Geography of the Ganges River." *ThoughtCo*, 24 May 2022, thoughtco.com. Accessed 15 Mar. 2022.
16. "Lakes." *Kerala Heritage*, n.d., keralaheritage.org. Accessed 15 Mar. 2022.
17. "Andrott." *U.T. Administration of Lakshadweep*, n.d., lakshadweep.gov.in. Accessed 2 Apr. 2022.
18. "Five Wettest Places in India You Should Know about." *India Today*, 19 June 2015, indiatoday.in. Accessed 2 Apr. 2022.
19. "India—Climate and Geography." *Working Abroad*, n.d., workingabroad.com. Accessed 2 Apr. 2022.

CHAPTER 3. PLANTS AND ANIMALS

1. Riley Fortier. "Why the Lotus Flower Is a Plant Celebrity." *PlantSnap*, 4 Apr. 2019, plantsnap.com. Accessed 3 Apr. 2022.
2. Nikki Tilley. "Growing a Banyan Tree." *Gardening Know-How*, 27 Apr. 2021, gardeningknowhow.com. Accessed 3 Apr. 2022.
3. Michelle Konstantinovsky. "The Mighty Banyan Tree Can 'Walk' and Live for Centuries." *HowStuffWorks*, 5 Apr. 2021, science.howstuffworks.com. Accessed 3 Apr. 2022.
4. Rolando Y. Wee. "Countries with the Most Threatened Plant Species." *World Atlas*, 25 Apr. 2017, mail.worldatlas.com. Accessed 3 Apr. 2022.
5. Konstantinovsky, "The Mighty Banyan Tree."
6. Shreya Pothula. "We Humans Have a Role to Play in Endangering These Rare Indian Trees." *SocialStory*, 9 May 2021, yourstory.com. Accessed 3 Apr. 2022.
7. "About the Asian Elephant." *World Wildlife Fund*, n.d., wwfindia.org. Accessed 3 Apr. 2022.
8. "Asian Elephant: Facts." *World Wildlife Fund*, n.d., worldwildlife.org. Accessed 3 Apr. 2022.
9. "Sloth Bear." *Smithsonian's National Zoo & Conservation Biology Institute*, n.d., nationalzoo.si.edu. Accessed 3 Apr. 2022.
10. "Red Panda." *National Geographic*, n.d., nationalgeographic.com. Accessed 3 Apr. 2022.
11. "Asiatic Lion." *World Wildlife Fund*, n.d., wwfindia.org. Accessed 3 Apr. 2022.
12. "Sundarbans National Park." *Global Alliance of National Parks*, n.d., national-parks.org. Accessed 5 Apr. 2022.
13. "National Endangered Species Day 2020: Here Are 7 Endangered Animal Species in India." *India Today*, 15 May 2020, indiatoday.in. Accessed 5 Apr. 2022.
14. "National Endangered Species Day 2020," *India Today*.
15. Ananya Bhattacharya. "The Rabies Crisis Plaguing India's Street Dogs Is about to Take a Turn for the Worse." *Quartz India*, 25 June 2021, qz.com. Accessed 5 Apr. 2022.

CHAPTER 4. HISTORY

1. "Who Were the Indus People?" *BBC*, n.d., bbc.co.uk. Accessed 7 Apr. 2022.
2. Avantika Lal. "Chandragupta Maurya." *World History Encyclopedia*, 4 Feb. 2019, worldhistory.org. Accessed 7 Apr. 2022.
3. Chandrika Kaul. "From Empire to Independence: The British Raj in India 1858–1947." *BBC*, 3 Mar. 2011, bbc.co.uk. Accessed 7 Apr. 2022.
4. Richard Cavendish. "The Amritsar Massacre." *History Today*, 4 Apr. 2009, historytoday.com. Accessed 7 Apr. 2022.
5. "Bringing Down an Empire: Gandhi and Civil Disobedience." *Constitutional Rights Foundation*, n.d., crf-usa.org. Accessed 7 Apr. 2022.

SOURCE **NOTES** CONTINUED

CHAPTER 5. PEOPLE AND CULTURE

1. Aaron O'Neill. "India: Estimated Total Population from 2016 to 2026." *Statista*, 27 Oct. 2021, statista.com. Accessed 10 Apr. 2022.
2. "India Area and Population Density." *World Population Review*, n.d., worldpopulationreview.com. Accessed 10 Apr. 2022.
3. "More than 19,500 Mother Tongues Spoken in India: Census." *Indian Express*, 1 July 2018, indianexpress.com. Accessed 10 Apr. 2022.
4. "About Hindi." *University of Illinois*, n.d., linguistics.illinois.edu. Accessed 10 Apr. 2022.
5. "More than 19,500 Mother Tongues Spoken in India," *Indian Express*.
6. "Bengali Speaking Countries." *WorldData.info*, n.d., worlddata.info. Accessed 10 Apr. 2022.
7. Angela Stephanou. "Top 10 Most Popular Indian Languages." *Pangea Translation Experts*, 19 June 2019, pangea.global.
8. Bhadriraju Krishnamurti. "Telugu Language." *Encyclopedia Britannica*, n.d., britannica.com. Accessed 10 Apr. 2022.
9. "Marathi." *University of Chicago: South Asian Languages and Civilizations*, n.d., salc.uchicago.edu. Accessed 10 Apr. 2022.
10. "10,000-Plus Growth in Sanskrit Speakers." *Telegraph*, 16 July 2016, telegraphindia.com. Accessed 10 Apr. 2022.
11. "India." *CIA World Factbook*, 7 June 2022, cia.gov. Accessed 10 Apr. 2022.

CHAPTER 6. POLITICS

1. "Military Size by Country 2022." *World Population Review*, n.d., worldpopulationreview.com. Accessed 12 Apr. 2022.
2. Sanyukta Kanwal. "Number of Sailors in Indian Naval Force as of 2019, by Type." *Statista*, 16 Mar. 2022, statista.com. Accessed 12 Apr. 2022.
3. "Indian Army Day 2021." *Business Insider*, 15 Jan. 2021, businessinsider.in. Accessed 12 Apr. 2022.

CHAPTER 7. ECONOMICS

1. Kimberly Amadeo. "India's Economy, Its Challenges, Opportunities, and Impact." *Balance*, 30 Aug. 2020, thebalance.com. Accessed 12 Apr. 2022.
2. Sanyukta Kanwal. "Agriculture in India—Statistics & Facts." *Statista*, 14 Feb. 2022, statista.com. Accessed 12 Apr. 2022.
3. "How One Farmer Built a Dairy Dynasty in India." *Forbes*, 18 Aug. 2016, forbes.com. Accessed 12 Apr. 2022.
4. "Tourism & Hospitality Industry in India." *IBEF*, n.d., ibef.org. Accessed 12 Apr. 2022.
5. "India Tourism Statistics 2019." *Ministry of Tourism*, n.d., tourism.gov.in. Accessed 12 Apr. 2022.
6. "Spices Industry and Export in India." *IBEF*, n.d., ibef.org. Accessed 12 Apr. 2022.
7. "India Coal." *Worldometer*, n.d., worldometers.info. Accessed 12 Apr. 2022.
8. Joshua W. Busby, Sarang Shidore, Johannes Urpelainen, and Morgan D. Bazilian. "The Case for US Cooperation with India on a Just Transition away from Coal." *Brookings Institution*, 20 Apr. 2021, brookings.edu. Accessed 12 Apr. 2022.
9. "Longest National Highways in India." *Reliance General*, n.d., reliancegeneral.co.in. Accessed 12 Apr. 2022.
10. "Mountain Railways of India." *UNESCO*, n.d., whc.unesco.org. Accessed 12 Apr. 2022.
11. "Road Infrastructure in India." *India Brand Equity Foundation*, n.d., ibef.org. Accessed 12 Apr. 2022.
12. "Road Infrastructure in India," *India Brand Equity Foundation*.

CHAPTER 8. INDIA TODAY

1. "Divorce Rate in India." *Advocate Khoj*, n.d., advocatekhoj.com. Accessed 12 Apr. 2022.

2. Soutik Biswas. "What Divorce and Separation Tell Us about Modern India." *BBC*, 29 Sept. 2016, bbc.com. Accessed 12 Apr. 2022.

3. Sanyukta Kanwal. "Rate of Female Labor Force Participation India 1990–2020." *Statista*, 16 Mar. 2022, statista.com. Accessed 12 Apr. 2022.

4. Sai Manish. "Coronavirus Impact: Over 100 Million Indians Could Fall below the Poverty Line." *Business Standard*, 17 Apr. 2020, business-standard.com. Accessed 20 July 2022.

5. "The Ganges: River of Life, Religion and Pollution." *Geographical*, 20 Jan. 2022, geographical.co.uk. Accessed 12 Apr. 2022.

6. "Tracking Coronavirus in India: Latest Map and Case Count." *New York Times*, 22 June 2022, nytimes.com. Accessed 20 July 2022.

7. "Tracking Coronavirus in India," *New York Times*.

8. Rama Venkat. "Two Years after World's Biggest Lockdown, India Surges Back to Normal Life." *Reuters*, 2 Mar. 2022, reuters.com. Accessed 12 Apr. 2022.

INDEX

ABOUT THE **AUTHOR**

TAMMY GAGNE

Tammy Gagne has written hundreds of books for both adults and children. Some of her recent books are about the US states of Pennsylvania and Texas. She lives in northern New England with her husband, son, and dogs.